P9-ECJ-515

looking over hills

looking over hills

by david kherdian

ILLUSTRATED BY NONNY HOGROGIAN

the giligia press / lyme center, new hampshire

Grateful acknowledgment is made to the following magazines
and anthology, where most of these poems were first pub-
lished: The Nation, Granite, The Minnesota Review, The
Lamp In the Spine, Apple, The Sage, Stations, and The
Berkshire Anthology.

books by david kherdian

POETRY

Looking Over Hills

Homage to Adana

On the Death of My Father and Other Poems

PROSE

Six San Francisco Poets

EDITOR

Visions of America: by the Poets of Our Time (with James Baloian) Down at the Santa Fe Depot: 20 Fresno Poets

BIBLIOGRAPHY

Six Poets of the San Francisco Renaissance: Portraits and Checklists

A Bibliography of William Saroyan: 1934–1964

NOTE

The poems in *Looking Over Hills* were written from 4 July to 4 August, 1970 in the Massachusetts Berkshires—on the grounds of Windsor Mountain School in Lenox, and on Cherry Hill Farm in Stockbridge.

The poems in *Stray Leaves* are an accumulation of poems from my first four years as a poet, 1967–1970, that for one reason or another I didn't wish to include in my first two books, or in section I of this book. They appear here in the order in which they were written.

D. K.

contents

looking over hills

1 looking over hills

two pennies found on the gravel
walk to windsor mountain school

TAKE ONE:

They are next to each other:
one forward, one back,
like an Oriental couple
out on a walk.

If more people didn't stay home
I'd be rich.

TAKE TWO:

I think I'll rub them together
to see if they will clean or
bring luck, before writing this poem.

for bill wehner

In Ionian garden
dog sits under lion paw
student in country school
flicks flies from blond curls
sits above seat on flat
new throne a-crumble
with a peach gone sun
on it all quietly
this dusk.

the couple

FOR ANNE HEMENWAY

Above the sloping lawn
and bordering trees,
rolling hills move from dark
to light to outlined mist

and off in the corner of the
picture the eye makes

they are still the color
the sun left, their soft
gestures as quiet as the breeze
that softly moves
among the leaves
and her fallen hair.

over hills into berkshire pines

Only here, where the trees
give to the wind its sound—
lush, flushed a deepening green,
that shades into the distance
into black, where all things are
hidden, giving birth, and coming
back: wings of blown pollen and
seed and oxygen-giving life.

in berkshire pines

Not one fir tree here, but
many. They make gardens with
their sizes. Their shapes are
the forms that families make.

Haphazard, deliberate,
planned in a row,
or carried by bird wing & beak,
they are in love with a
distant mind.

Always, everywhere, a tree not
pine, and a squirrel in its
branches caught by the sun.

The walk of the people is bent
into a circle and this is
their dance.

squirrels in wind pine

Squirrels from treetops listen to
pine wind song. Such overtures of
the season come again and again,
and today, after cloud change and
light rain, the heavy tender wind
comes to pine grove for lute song,
and to comb back animal hair.

Yesterday, the squirrels played all
afternoon in the sun. Today they
are silent among old leaves and
branches, safe in their nests.

In quiet, they give their secrets
over to the earth, and take them back.

in spring green berkshire rain

It was the night in coming, moving
down from mountains into pine. In
the morning the starlings clustered
on the grass, held hardly moving
in a trance.

This is the hour the trees know
best: they honor the rain by
holding fast. At the first drizzle
they raise their voices to the wind
that bends and sways their branches
back.

pines: a poem

Fallen to the ground
or growing from
seed to sapling
fir to fallen cone,
its branches give
a jagged shade; its
undergrowth of ferns
and moist brown pounded
earth provide substance
for a tiny world of lives
we see and cannot see.

The spirit of the tree
is happy and shimmers
for what it knows.

the instant

I cannot see two squirrels playing
in a tree in sunlight, holding on
to bark and hiding each from each,
without wanting to reach my hand
up to their furred bodies and know
again such tenderness, and feel
their innocence across my back.

For an emptied instant I hold time
in the cupped brows of my thought
and I am freed at last from the
insane wars of the mind and heart.

clouds: a poem

Grey skies shrink tree shadows.
Animals crouch and wait, while
birds keep calling one another
back. The time is held for what
cannot move; it holds and grows
from where it stands: the green
hour that trees and grass can
understand.

when these old barns lost
their inhabitants and then
their pain and then all semblance
of determined human construction

1.
They began to sway to the
forms of nature, desiring
some final ruin; desiring
some final ruin and return

2.
Their bodies ache and sway
to the rhythms of the
beckoning hills

3.
They carry in their burnt
wood the descending rays
of the setting sun

4.
Their windows are as small
as eyes

5.
They wish again to be a
falling tree

sunflower

You stand humble and mighty
and so overwhelmed by your
own light, that you must bow,
the sun-drenched pollen dancer,
leaping solemnly from the
rock bed weed patch that
gives you—O so many secrets,
and all their time.

cherry hill farm

I sit on the dead stump
below the fox burrow,
among bad and good berries,
and thorns, and strange grasses
or weeds.

A frightened grasshopper
jumps out of sight and then
ascends a twig. We are both
stillfully silent: I remembering
my youth, watching him, he
frightful of my presence,
though I have been gone some
thirty years.

II   stray leaves

a poem for cats and birds

Sun already set at my back
    he sits on the green cool lawn
    beside my feet
Content, quiet, but sniffing the air,
    he begins to make throat sounds
    only I can hear,
while the mockingbird concealed
    in the bush
clatters an army full of
    challenging sounds.
Not exactly a game, and he is not
    entirely dismayed
but soon they will become
    mutual enemies
and then Sirak will leave my
    feet
and venture forth
to stalk his karma

lately richard brautigan isn't enough

In Dundee
        orange marmalade
        comes in a jar
handsome enough to hold
        pencils & letteropeners
        and other nice things.
And I should mention
        Keiller, too, and his son.
They established it in 1797

love poem / for virginia and sirak

You are lying outside on
    your stomach
reading a book
    I am reading some poems
the cracked pomegranate
    you left
on the kitchen counter
    I finished
just a moment ago
    when the door slammed

the cat is walking
    outside the
window under my book
    towards where you lie
and will soon come
    to you
because you have
    not looked up
and spoken his name

my mother and the hummingbird

As the green-winged hummingbird
　　darts sideways into the
　　leaves of our baby apricot tree
Suspended, taking sugar with his
　　quivering bill
I move in around the palm tree
　　to have a better look
But my mother pushes open
　　the window and says
　　right now write a poem.

poem for sirak

the palm leaf
fans to the earth
   and stops
to hold in the mouth
of its teeth
and the shadow
of its tongue

   a sleeping cat
coated in dust
and warmth

it becomes this for me

rain-soaked leaves
that twirling fall
mark the path
the cat will walk,
as he steps from
the curb,
coming from hurt
to healing to home;
and the cars that
push waters in sprays
of reflecting colors,
everything suddenly a
metallic blue;
whirring wheels
their own special noise;
or whatever else
I see from the window
or that comes to me
from beneath the door,
because I have embraced
the silence of a slowly
turning life in the
adopted valley of
my home

29:x:69

the caterpillar shivers
on the green leaf

on the porch
a dead bee

a live wind whirls
crimson flowers

leaf grass and seed
move and turn in departure

poem in april

FOR LEPHIA AND TONY FUDGE

I have waited, watching daily
the tangled Monterey Moss around
the base of the tree on my
neighbor's lawn. Today,
it blossomed pink and formed
a counterpart to the delicate
green leaves of the Silver Tip Maple.
Wherever you are, if you can imagine
it you are there: close your eyes
and try to see.

a poem for my father

It isn't much to remember—
you've been gone more than 12 years;
I only occasionally go home, and
seldom for more than a day
when I do.
The city is changing, getting older,
slowly dying—and it's so hard
to see anything give way and begin
to go, because you know whatever
goes must go for good.
And it is funny what you do remember,
because better than any poem
we rose early, and while I readied
the poles & lines & bait, you made
our sandwich lunch, and then we walked
to Lake Michigan, up Prospect Street,
thru Umbaji Park and the coal yards,
and then thru the factories, one
by one, where we stopped and stood
together, man and boy, father and son,
and man to man we pissed against
the factory walls.

at bob totten's

Bluejay sits on cottonwood limb
above lady in rubber gloves
cutting weeds.
Daughter in sun flower dress says:
"I was helping dollie up the steps"—
looks at Bluejay and keeps talking;
snip, snip, wing flap, sound of
sneakers on porch descending.

for anne

It is your doe-eyed moon-shaped face,
your unkempt apartment with the
pleasurable accidents that
carelessness brings, and your funky
records that you leave playing
after you leave, to inform the
anguished silences we live in,
or as an invitation, in case you
are out (an unwritten note that
you will be back soon, please come in),
that all come together when I see you
below your window, barefooted,
slung-pursed, in your denim shirt
and tattered dress, and know you are
the refugee of the mended valentine
of a heartbroken love.

26:VII:70

A sudden vermillion flash
among the sun-struck leaves,
against the light blue sky.

Beautiful Baltimore Oriole!

A shy celebrity
as strange as Sweeney,
high in the treetops.

the siamese cat

The yellow bedspread
he sleeps upon
is slowly changing
to the gentle quiet
gold of his breath.

1250 copies of this book were published in November, 1972. The book was designed by Nonny Hogrogian in 10 pt Century Expanded and printed on Strathmore Artlaid paper. Of this number 1000 copies are bound in paper wrappers; 200 copies in cloth; and 50 numbered copies in variant cloth binding have been signed by poet and artist.